Form

Carl Potter was born in Beverley, East Yorkshire, in 1984, and remained there until starting a degree in English and Creative Writing at Leeds Trinity University College.

He has had a variety of jobs, including landscape gardener and chef, but has always written poetry and fiction. *Form* marks the first time his work has been published in a single volume.

Form

CARL POTTER

VALLEY

FORM

First published in 2012
by Valley Press
Woodend, The Crescent, Scarborough, YO11 2PW
www.valleypressuk.com

Printed in England by Imprint Digital,
Upton Pyne, Exeter

© 2012 Carl Potter
All rights reserved

The right of Carl Potter to be identified as author
of this work has been asserted in accordance with Section
77 of the Copyright, Designs and Patents Act 1988

*This book is sold subject to the condition that it shall not,
by way of trade or otherwise, be lent, resold, hired out,
or otherwise circulated without the publisher's prior
consent in any form of binding or cover other than that
in which it is published and without a similar condition,
including this condition, being imposed on the
subsequent purchaser.*

ISBN: 978-1-908853-03-5
Cat. no.: VP0022

A catalogue record for this book
is available from the British Library

www.valleypressuk.com/authors/carlpotter

9 8 7 6 5 4 3 2 1

CONTENTS

Explaining to Joshua Why Snowmen Have to Melt 11
Ghosts 12
Mandrake 13
Golden 14
Lesser Spotted Lockheed Martin 15
Poor Horsforth 16
Rep 18
Imperfect German 19
Midnight Movie Heroin 20
Tiger Hunt 21
Walter Mitty Character 22
Stock Market Crash 24
The Resistance of Memory 25
You Left Your Shoes 26

I'd like to say thanks to my family, my friends,
and to Paul, Martyn, Sue, Jim, Amina,
and all the lecturing staff at Leeds Trinity.

Special thanks are due to Gerald Onn,
for assistance with the German translation on page 19.

for J & C

Explaining to Joshua Why Snowmen Have to Melt

How cruel the winter,
when your hands, so cold with frost
braved its bite to bring it life.
So gentle was your touch,
the sacrifice of bloody fingers,
frozen knees, and smiling.
How proud you were;
childish pride, too pure for vanity.

A searching hand that found my own
and brought me to the garden,
shook with hope and revelation.
'Look what I did. Look at his nose!
Look at his eyes! Look at his toes!'
Salted rain upon the ground,
a heart to warm the season.

Our victory was fantasy,
snowblind I and loveblind boy.
A searching hand that found my own,
is shaking in the garden:
'Where's he gone?'
An empty sky, with whipping cirrus,
birds that cry, as if they see us,
boy and I.

How cruel was our winter.

Ghosts

The last days of the Bodmin beast
will end before the spring.
The sycophantic water-rats
are sharpening their teeth.
Mystery to history;
the shadows in the black
will hitherto be brought to light and burned upon our reason.

Hunter in the autumn, mother in the harvest
to honeysuckled greedy mouths that barely know it's there.
This will be its fortune, every bird a silhouette.
To hear the slapping pigeon wing
and fear the flying axe.
As if the creature knows it.
In shame, the staggered death,
because it bore the joyful claws that tore within itself.

Mandrake

He stands again
      limp
blades
      between pink
white
fingers.

Golden

Hole of gold, apart from time
held open by exotic matter.
No matter that the patter
of tiny feet
closed the circle.
Love you, Au,
I do.

Eternally old hardened hoop.
A cheer, a whoop then given back.
Refuge in a toolbox.
Visits copper cousins
in a dirty, dusty corner.

Strange coldy coldness;
since furnace forged, soon forgotten.
Buried beneath an apple tree,
plumps the second season's fruit.

Superhero shiny ting!
In summer sunlight,
swells the bosom of reflected pride.
Blinded worms within.

Goaded by fashion
into empty reluctance,
and limping on forever,
to melt before
a million birthday candles.

Lesser Spotted Lockheed Martin

Out of the lazy, melting sunset, come the eagles.
Indifferent, insouciant, soaring on thermals.
Gliding home in a nowhere sky.
Ignore the war below.

Little devils! Susurrus assassins.
In the shadow of the eagle wing
is where they play their genocide.

Benevolent, smiling killers.

Black mist of biting midges.
Lightning bird cuts a clean arc of nothingness.
It slowly seeps back,
the lost soon forgotten.

The sound of terror, tearing on the edge of a feather
like a backwards gasp.
Slicing linear notes;
the ambience of summer.

Red sunlight reflects from a thousand falling wings.

They climb towards the eagles now,
relaxed parabolas.
Exchanging tweets of satiated glee.
The sky falls silent as they turn to the south,
where black water melts on a black horizon.

Poor Horsforth

It's a cancer;
the tumourous tendrils
of the city
pierce sandstone walls and pedestrian sentiments
of surrounding hamlets.

Here comes doctor and the medics
to streamline proactive solutions
and start its silent heart with
a social-regen-project.

Clock-stopping neon narcotic
streams down concrete veins.
Heart to extremities, rotting though they are,
glowing plastic poison into the tips.

Doctor, we're losing him,
the vital signs are flatlining!
Give me forty cc's of heritage stat!
Put plaques on the houses, drain the people,
put them in jars.
Flood it with formaldehyde.

Mrs Smith's pantry;
a ticket booth for tourists with
a little list of prices upon her frozen breast.
Just watch the mourners roll in.
Camera flash; bored children point at dates from long ago,
and pay their last respects.

The coffin is closed, the rich folk leave.
The town's mouth smiles, the town's eyes close.
The town's mind drifts
and dreams of when its heartbeat was its own.

Rep

Riff raff karma bums and fellows of the season
         singing roundelay,
                  madrigal and odelay.
Posing with acoustic horns,
reciting to the sun.

To love the rut in cloying blood, with sharp and dirty antlers.

But when the moon, that dripping moon,
that cloying, guilty, licking moon?

The waiting moon will swell and burst.
Too late will come the darkness
and the chance to carve reflections
in the sand.

Once more unto the beach,
         whorled and savaged.
When the salvage is boiled,
there remains a scum
         effervescent oil,
rusty scarred metal,
a simple love of fire
and hollowing blues.

Riff raff karma bums and fellows of the season
         singing roundelay,
                  madrigal and odelay.
Posing with acoustic horns,
reciting to the sun.

Imperfect German

In my hand I hold your sepia grin,
as you sip at cold tea, talking to me
over blackened photographs of the sea;
stories of heroes, courage and gin.

In a dented jubilee biscuit tin,
love letters from old Germany.
Papier Blitz vernichtet sympathie,
covered by smiles as thin as your skin.

'*Krankenschwester Schwartz*' injects insulin.
Hakenkreuz auf foto hides beneath me.
You lie, and say that you are sleepy.
Ich bringe dich zumm bett. She tucks you in.

Du gibst einen gruß! with dirty fingers.
She lowers your hand and smiles at the pain.
You smile with your teeth, the fat nurse lingers.
Ich küsse dich tschüß and leave you again.

Midnight Movie Heroin

The moonlight's blushes; fire on skin
        burning kisses on the heart
and scorching scars
bereft,
between the moonlight dances
kisses part.

Sunfire follows the moonfire dance
and washes the blushes away,
        and fractures the shadows
so carefully cast.
So cast to the death of the day.

The dance, the burn!
Caressing fire
        maudlin secrets
darkling desire.
The flame of the moonlight
            blood on the fire
and blushes and kisses return.

Tiger Hunt

Cold arresting rushes
bind her feet together.
Keep her toes in uniform;
hiding in the marshes.

A hunting tooth, a fractured bone.
The shock of claws on feather,

will silence all with hunger
or fracture bones, the hidden bones
with hidden claws, the hidden claws.

A featherburst of hidden bones are lost among the
    marshes.

Exterminate the marshes!
The hidden claws, the fractured bones.
The dead within the uniform
and cold arresting rushes.

Walter Mitty Character

Say hello to my little friend.
In his day he was the bitches' bastard.
Now he just lies there like an unemployed whale.
'I coulda been a contender, I coulda been a somebody.
But as soon as I get out they pull me back in!'
We all go a little crazy sometimes.
But this goes to eleven.
The Goddamn plane has crashed into the mountain.
Come on Tommy, this isn't us. We're not like these animals.
If we don't leave now we'll never make it...

'They're heeeere!
They've breached the perimeter and they're closing fast.
Soon it will be too late!'

They shot him, they shot Tommy. I mean they whacked him.

'I'm dying man! Oh God, I'm fucking dying!
You finally did it. You maniacs!
Go! Go on without me.'

And he died, man. He died right in my arms.
I was scared of what they'd do to me, so I ran.
And I just kept on running, and running.
What will they say? Will they say he was a good man, a kind man? Wrong!
He was one of a kind, too weird to live, too unique to die.

But that was back in the old country.
I've been holed up here ever since.

I'm thinking everything's different now, everything's changed.
This abuse of my body must stop, every muscle must be tight.
As soon as I get out of here, I'm gonna find you.
I will find you. I will find you and I will kill you.
I'm number one. King fucking Kong!
I will end you. Do you hear me? I will end you.
Everyone!

'Open the door.
Open the door, HAL
Open the door, HAL
Open the door
Open the door HAL
Open the door...'

Stock Market Crash

He wraps the ticker tape around his neck,
checks the dials on his Omega watch.
He tucks good luck charms into his pocket.
His shiny shoe kicks a fat pigeon.
He gazes down at the ground below,
spits champagne at the London air.
He steps into worldly oblivion.

As he crashes to the concrete floor
the trailing tape coils around him,
buries his corpse in yards of pink nonsense.
A speculating spectator walks by,
casts a quick glance at the pile of numbers;
the final, end of day trading receipt,
and decides to invest in Lithium.

The Resistance of Memory

Remember the bushes?
That spring green bubble,
outside of time,
inside of us?
It's still there.

Remember the carving
of names on a branch?
Our words and ideas,
illegible letters?
They're still there.

Remember the sunset?
Sticky sycamore dew
dry on summer skin.
Discarded cigarettes?
They're still there.

Remember the kisses?
Musty autumn mud smell
rising from our feet.
Mirrored shoe-prints?
They're still there.

Remember the winter?
Silent snow
settling on us, gently.
Remember when it melted?

You Left Your Shoes

You left your shoes
dead on the stairs.
Right heel points home,
left heel to hell.
Heaven then hell.

Your morning skin.
Ghosts of kisses,
tight little circles,
tight little secrets.
Taste on my tongue.

Shameful shower,
wash me away,
won't go away,
can't go away.
Kiss me again.

Pick up the shoes,
turn on the stairs,
promise you can't
kiss me again.
Then tomorrow.